THE WORLD'S CITIES

ROME

CREDITS

Series Editor: Nicolas Wright
Series Designer: Kris Flynn
Picture Researcher: Kathy Brandt

Text by Michael Gibson

Commissioned Photographs by
Anne-Marie Erhlich

Published by Chartwell Books Inc., A
Division of Book Sales Inc., 110 Enterprise
Avenue, Secaucus, New Jersey 07094

© Marshall Cavendish Limited 1978

Produced by Theorem Publishing Limited,
71/73 Great Portland Street, London W1N 5DH
for Marshall Cavendish Books Limited

Printed in Great Britain

First printing 1978

ISBN 0 89009 161 7

THE WORLD'S CITIES
ROME

CHARTWELL
BOOKS INC.

CONTENTS

Introduction to Rome

About 3000 years ago groups of shepherd-farmers settled on the semi-circle of hills overlooking the Italian coastal plain of Latium. Later, these early settlers started to move down onto the plain. Fifteen miles from the mouth of the River Tiber they found a deep valley containing seven hills: the Palatium, Cermalus, Fagutal, Oppius, Cispius, Aventine and Caelian. This site attracted the newcomers because it was well-watered and protected and commanded a possible river crossing midway between the coast and the hills. From the wattle and daub village of these early Latins arose what was to become the mightiest city in the western world.

During the course of the next 28 centuries, Rome earned its title as the Eternal City. As the co-founder with Ancient Greece of western civilization, it enjoyed a great Silver Age of poetry and prose, and painting and sculpture. Its master architects produced the incomparable Forum Romanum and the splendid palaces of the Palatine. As the home of the Popes it became the religious centre of western Europe, adorned with a breathtaking collection of great churches and religious art: the Rome of Michelangelo, Bernini and so many others, still lives and breathes. In the same way, Rome is still the city that attracted the 18th-century travellers on their Grand Tour and the reluctant capital of the newly founded Italian state.

This book illustrates all these aspects of Rome's history, as well as creating a lively picture of the city as it is today: the Rome of great crowded squares and fountains; of romantic bridges; of noisy markets and chic shops; of delicious food and *la dolce vita*. Like all great cities, Rome has as many faces as a multi-faceted diamond.

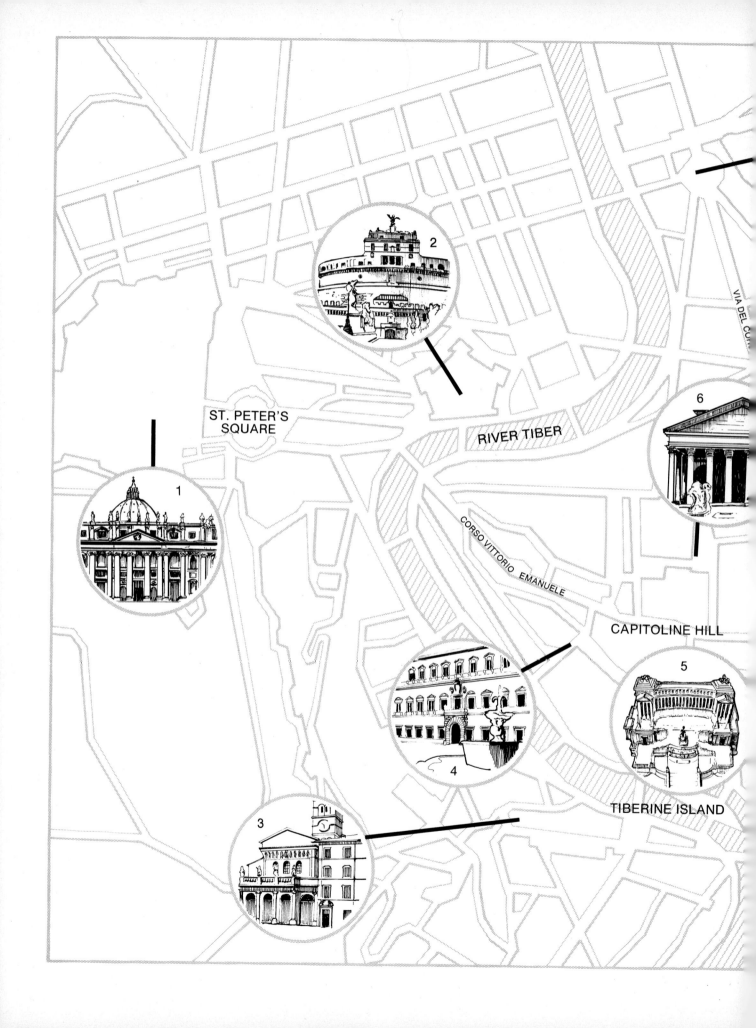

ST. PETER'S
SQUARE

RIVER TIBER

CORSO VITTORIO EMANUELE

VIA DEL CO...

CAPITOLINE HILL

TIBERINE ISLAND

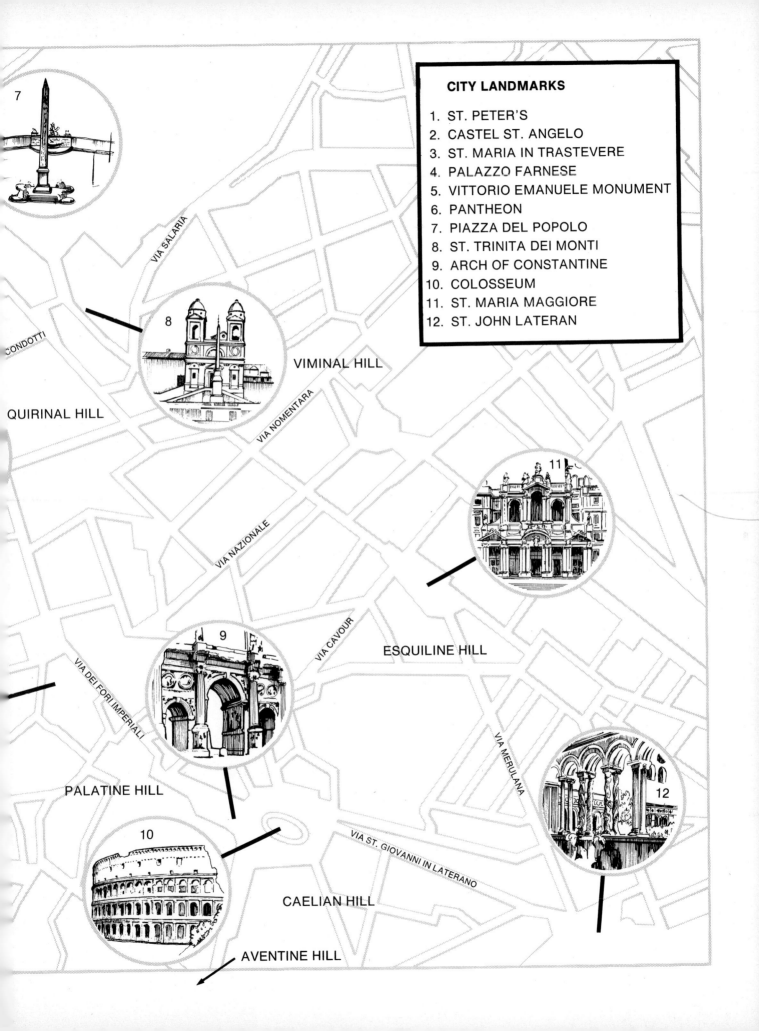

CITY LANDMARKS

1. ST. PETER'S
2. CASTEL ST. ANGELO
3. ST. MARIA IN TRASTEVERE
4. PALAZZO FARNESE
5. VITTORIO EMANUELE MONUMENT
6. PANTHEON
7. PIAZZA DEL POPOLO
8. ST. TRINITA DEI MONTI
9. ARCH OF CONSTANTINE
10. COLOSSEUM
11. ST. MARIA MAGGIORE
12. ST. JOHN LATERAN

VIA SALARIA

CONDOTTI

QUIRINAL HILL

VIMINAL HILL

VIA NOMENTARA

VIA NAZIONALE

ESQUILINE HILL

VIA CAVOUR

VIA DEI FORI IMPERIALI

PALATINE HILL

VIA MERULANA

VIA ST. GIOVANNI IN LATERANO

CAELIAN HILL

AVENTINE HILL

The Eternal City

Rome has been the focal point of the western world for most of its 2700 year history. Its origins are lost in myth and legend. Was the city founded by the twins Romulus and Remus, in about 753 BC and occupied by a colony of Latins? Or was it created by a mysterious band of exiles from Asia Minor, as Virgil suggested in his epic poem, *Aeneid?* As yet there is no clear-cut answer to this question.

What we do know, however, is that during Rome's crucial formative years it was dominated by the Etruscans. Very little has been learned about these superb soldier-craftsmen, their language has yet to be translated. However, their artefacts suggest a people of great sophistication and power. The Romans owed this ancient race an enormous debt because their triumphs were built upon a culture and technology acquired, at least in part, from them.

After the expulsion of Tarquin the Proud, the last of Rome's kings, in 510 BC, the city became a republic, ruled by the Senate and people as the legend on its famous seal proclaims: SPQR – *Senatus populusque romanus.* While a complicated constitution and body of law slowly evolved, the Roman army rapidly grew in power. The dynamic city state quickly extended its frontiers to include the Latins, Etruscans, Samnites, Lucanians and the Greek settlers in southern Italy. No sooner had the Italic peoples been absorbed than the Romans turned their restless attention to the conquest of Sicily, Carthage, Spain and Greece in the period between 340 and 133 BC.

In the early days of the Republic the city consisted of an assortment of evil-smelling hovels perched on the Palatine Hill, in the Suburra and along the left bank of the River Tiber. The basis of Roman society was the ancestor-venerating family, ruled by an all-powerful paterfamilias. The families were divided into clans (gentes) with common names, gods and burial places. Cattle ranching on the rich pasture land by the river gave way to agriculture and the rise of the peasant farmer. Gradually, Roman society became divided into Patricians and Plebeians; the latter had already compelled the former to recognize their representatives, the tribunes of the people, by 450 BC.

In Republican times, the hub of Roman life was the Forum, an oblong space of about two and a half acres surrounded by shops. The Temple of Vesta, the goddess of the hearth and family, and the House of the Vestal Virgins stood on one side of the complex in the shadow of the Capitoline Hill. On the other side loomed the imposing shape of the Regia, the house of the Pontifex Maximus, the High Priest. The Senate building stood in the north-east corner. Traversing the area was the Via Sacra, a winding road along which triumphal processions passed on their way to the Capitoline.

The Via Veneto with the Excelsior Hotel and palm trees in the foreground. This street is famous for its hotels, cafes and nightspots.

8

The most dramatic developments on the Palatine Hill took place during the Imperial Period when the early emperors competed with each other to build the most impressive and extravagant palace complex. The summit was covered with the houses of Augustus, Tiberius, Caligula, Domitian, Hadrian, and most magnificent of all, that of Septimus Severus. His rose in seven massive stages along the southern flanks of the hill. In addition, the Palatine possessed a beautiful stadium, several temples set in gardens, the Halls of Justice and a barracks for the Praetorian Guard. Across the valley, the Oppian Hill was almost completely covered by Nero's Golden House.

Below: The Via dei Fori Imperiali runs in a straight line to the Piazza del Colosseo. This magnificent street, lined with trees and flower gardens, was opened in October 1933 as the Via dell' Impero. On its right lies the Roman Forum and other Imperial Fora.

Right: Part of the aqueduct built by Domitian to provide water for his palace on the Palatine Hill. It was an extension of the Aqua Claudia which ran from the Caelian to the Palatine.

As the city grew in wealth and power, the Campus Martius became covered with baths and places of entertainment like the Theatre of Marcellus, much of which still stands as a splendid example of Roman monumental architecture. It was started by Julius Caesar and completed by Augustus in 11 BC; he named it after his nephew Marcellus, the son of Octavia. Further south on the site of part of Nero's demolished masterpiece, the Golden House, arose the Colosseum, the longest lasting testimony to Rome's greatness. Started by Vespasian, dedicated by Titus in AD 80 and completed by Domitian, it rang with the clash of gladiators' weapons, the roars of animals and the victims' screams throughout the Imperial Period.

By the reign of Constantine (306-337), Rome had a population of one million — 190 granaries and 250 corn mills supplied the city with flour; 150 fountains and eleven aqueducts provided it with water. There were eleven market-places, eleven baths, ten basilicas, two circuses, two amphitheatres and 28 libraries. The city was divided into quarters, criss-crossed by paved streets and deeply rutted by the wheels of heavy wagons and chariots, except where modern looking bollards barred the way. At the busy intersections, there were brightly coloured niches containing statues of the gods. In spite of the ever encroaching slums and the surprisingly modern looking apartment blocks, the city contained many beautiful gardens, rich with statues and fountains.

The rich still enjoyed life: working or receiving clients in the cool of the morning, taking a siesta at midday and exercising in the Campus Martius or one of the city's many gymnasia in the afternoon. On completing their exercises, young and old made their way to the baths to enjoy the sensual luxury of an elaborate cleansing rite. The baths were enormous architectural masterpieces equipped with brightly decorated reception rooms, steam rooms and a variety of water plunges ranging from the scaldingly hot to the icy cold. Clean, massaged, oiled and dressed in clean clothes, the Romans were ready for their main meal and social event of the day. This good life was only made possible by the toiling hordes of slaves. Some were abused and maltreated while others were prized for their skills. A few were even allowed to open their own businesses.

The ordinary people, who lived in the city's crowded tenement blocks and slums, worked in the busy fora, the narrow streets full of tanners, butchers, sword makers, barbers and numerous wine shops and eating houses, or on the busy wharfs of Ostia. The poor and destitute were reconciled to their lot by the provision of the proverbial bread and circuses. At night, the rich kept to their houses or the well-lit thoroughfares. The streets of Rome were infested with robbers and kidnappers, species of criminals that have flourished throughout the city's long history. Heavy carts rumbled through the streets, rocking from side to side, occasionally trapping the unwary against the walls.

By the time Constantine became Emperor in AD 306, the days of Ancient Rome's greatness were numbered. The vulnerability of the city to the attacks of the barbarians had already forced the Emperor Aurelian to build a great enclosure of fortified walls between AD 270 and 275. The authority of the old gods had been undermined by the spread of Christianity whose persecuted members were buried in the catacombs outside the city. Following Constantine's recognition of the Christian faith, churches sprang up on the sites of St Paul's outside the walls, St Sebastiano, St John Lateran and St Maria Maggiore. Long before Alaric the Visigoth's hordes appeared beneath the walls of Rome in 410, the city had been supplanted as the focus of political and economic power by Constantinople, Constantine's new capital, built on the site of the old Greek town of Byzantium on the Black Sea.

For several centuries Rome remained a magnet for the barbarian invaders. Each in turn hoped to find the world's accumulated wealth stored there. In the sixth century, the Byzantine Emperor Justinian made a spirited attempt to restore the western empire. All he succeeded in doing was creating a beleaguered province based on the city of Ravenna in north-east Italy, not Rome. During this period, as the once mighty city declined into a regional backwater, a new power arose within its crumbling walls, the power of the Papacy. Building assiduously upon the rock of its Petrine foundation, the Pope gradually established his supremacy over the bishops of western Europe. Then the Papacy looked round for a political defender to take the place of the defunct Roman Empire. First Pepin the Short and then Charles the Great were chosen for this role. After many years of vacillation, Charles, or Charlemagne as he was known, appeared in Rome in 800 and was crowned emperor in St Peter's on Christmas Day. A new empire, the Holy Roman Empire, had been born.

By the tenth century, Rome was a town of some 60000 souls, dominated by noble families who struggled with each other for control not only of the town but of the Papacy itself. Much of the vast area within the dilapidated walls was filled with orchards and fields where sheep and pigs roamed freely. The Forum had become a stone island in a sea of vegetation; plants pushed their way up between the flagstones and wrapped themselves around the cracking pillars, now stripped of most of their marble. Nevertheless the power of the Papacy continued to increase. During a titanic struggle over the right to appoint bishops, Pope Gregory VII first excommunicated, then humiliated Emperor Henry IV at the castle of Canossa where he begged the Pope's forgiveness. Even though Gregory later had to suffer the indignity of flight from the imperial armies closing in on Rome, and ended his life in exile among the Normans of southern Italy, he had established the Papacy as an independent force and had laid the foundations for even greater claims to authority over the laity.

The strengthened Papacy reached the apogee of its power during the reign of the subtle pontiff Innocent III, (1161-1216). He played a key part in launching the Fourth Crusade and then diverted its soldiers to the conquest of Constantinople and the Byzantine Empire. From this pinnacle of power, the Papacy steadily declined during the next two centuries into disrepute and relative impotence. Following bitter struggles among the Roman nobility, Clement V, in 1308, moved the Papal seat to Avignon in southern France, unintentionally inaugurating the period known as the Babylonish Captivity which lasted until 1378.

Below: Throughout the Middle Ages, Swiss pikemen were in great demand. In 1506, the Pope formed the Swiss Guard which retains its striking uniform, which is said to have been designed by Michelangelo.
Right: An altar in the Catacombs. The Catacombs are subterranean tufa quarries where the early Christians worshipped, took refuge from their persecutors and buried their dead.

While the Papacy was enduring these tribulations and slowly recovering from them, Italy was experiencing the first stages of the so-called Renaissance or rebirth of learning. The last years of the 15th and the first years of the 16th centuries were the golden age of Papal Rome. The city became the cultural centre of the western world once more, attracting the great artists of the period like Leonardo da Vinci, Michelangelo and Raphael. The Sistine Chapel was built and although decorated by a number of renowned painters remains dominated by Michelangelo's magnificent ceiling frescoes and the *Last Judgement.* St Peter's was rebuilt, its famous dome being the work of Bramante and Michelangelo, and a new city laid out. The Capitoline Square was dramatically altered. Michelangelo refaced the Palazzo Senatorio and the Palazzo dei Conservatori and built the Palazzo Nuovo to complete the unity of the complex. To emphasize the importance of the star patterned pavement, Michelangelo placed the equestrian statue of what was then thought to be Constantine the Great (actually Marcus Aurelius) at its centre.

Below left: The Church of St Maria in Cosmedin is distinguished by its bell-tower. Romanesque in style, this is one of the finest in Rome.

Right: Ponds and fountains were to be found everywhere in Ancient Rome as it was the custom for the rich to provide such amenities for all to enjoy.

Below: The Villa Guilia was built in 1550–1555 for Pope Julius III and houses a collection of pre-Roman antiquities. The courtyard contains this superb loggia.

While Rome was being transformed and beautified by the artists of the high Renaissance, the Papacy made its last attempt to play a dominant role in the political life of Europe. The era of the Italian Wars saw Italy invaded in the north by the armies of France and in the south by those of Spain. The Renaissance Popes tried desperately hard to maintain the balance of power and to preserve their own lands and influence by creating leagues and alliances. The result of this meddling in European politics was the devastating sack of Rome in 1527 by the unpaid and mutinous imperial troops.

A century later the Popes threw themselves into even more ambitious building programmes than their Renaissance predecessors. As a result the centre of Rome took on its present, distinctly baroque character. Under Paul V's patronage the great nave of St Peter's was added while the sculptor Bernini designed a tomb for Urban VIII (1623-1644). This became a model for all funeral monuments for more than 100 years. Bernini also covered the tomb of St Peter with the superb baldacchino or canopy, for which the Pantheon temple was stripped of its bronze ornaments. With the accession of Innocent X in 1644, Bernini fell from favour and Francesco Boromini and Alessandro Algardi became the dominant artistic influences. Innocent's greatest achievement was the Piazza Navona with its brilliant fountains. The Sienese Pope, Alexander VII (1645-1667), reinstated Bernini whose career reached its climax with the construction of the Cathedra Petri.

After the death of Clement IX in 1669, papal patronage declined rapidly, partly at least as a result of Urban VIII's profligacy. However, the 18th century saw the Papacy once more taking a vigorous interest in the arts. Various famous projects were set in motion: the Spanish Steps were built by De Sancti, the facade of the Lateran was created by Alessandro Galilei, and the Trevi Fountain brought to triumphant completion by Nicola Salvi. The Capitoline Museums were founded and the bases of their unique collections of Roman statuary laid down.

Left: The Piazza San Pietro was Bernini's masterpiece. The stupendous colonnade and fountain were completed for Alexander VII (1656–1667).
Below: The Spanish Steps are a popular area for artists and salesmen. Jewellery, leatherwork and paintings are the most popular commodities.

Music, drama and painting flourished under the enlightened patronage of Cardinal Pietro Ottoboni. Mid-century Rome was swamped by the rising tide of neo-classicism stimulated by the discovery of the ruins of Pompeii and Herculaneum in the 1730s and 1740s. The Villa Albani was built in the 1750s as an Imperial villa suburbana and lavishly adorned with antique marbles. The Borghese Palace was modernized by Antonio Asprucci. Throughout the 18th century more and more foreigners made Rome the focus of their Grand Tour. On their visits to the city, they not only imbibed the teachings of neo-classicism but laid the foundations of their own private collections of *objets d'art*. Rome became Europe's largest market for antiques and works of art.

The French Revolution in 1789 and Napoleon's later conquests upset the settled pattern of Italian and Roman political life. The Pope and the Italian royal families were exiled, at least for a time, and their people given some experience of self-government before they were absorbed into various Napoleonic systems. Although, on Napoleon's defeat, their old masters were reimposed upon the Italians, the forces calling

Above: The monument of Victor Emmanuel II, sometimes known as the wedding cake, is built of dazzling white Botticeno marble from Brescia and dominates the Piazza di Venezia. It was inaugurated in 1915.
Right: Trajan's Column was dedicated in AD 113 to the memory of the Emperor's conquest of the Dacians, the inhabitants of present-day Rumania. The Emperor's statue was replaced by one of St Peter in 1588.

20

for the Risorgimento had been released. After abortive revolutions in 1830 and 1848, an Italian state without Rome was established by a formidable triumvirate made up of Victor Emmanuel II of Piedmont-Sardinia, Count Camillo Cavour and Giuseppe Garibaldi. The Papacy remained secure within its walls as long as Napoleon III continued to garrison troops in Rome, but following their defeats in the Franco-Prussian War the French withdrew and Garibaldi's legion breached the walls and took possession of the city in the name of the new Italian state. Unhappily, this led to the severing of relations between the Papacy and the new regime: a state of affairs which continued until 1929 when Mussolini's Lateran Treaties at last healed the breach.

Below: The EUR, or Esposizione Universale di Roma, is twelve minutes' train journey from Rome. It was started in 1938 to the designs of Marcello Piacentini as a memorial to the achievements of Fascism. It was not completed until 1952 when various government offices were moved to the site and many museums were opened.
Right: A modern obelisk in the EUR.

From 1870, Rome became what she had never really ceased to be, the capital of Italy. Now, Piedmontese influence was added to those of Ancient Rome and the Papacy. A new quarter sprang up around the Piazza Vittorio Emmanuele II, a porticoed square which forms the hub of a series of straight thoroughfares intersecting at right angles. The unification of Italy was commemorated by the controversial Victor Emmanuel monument, or the wedding cake, as some irreverent Romans call it. It was the outcome of an architectural competition won by Giuseppe Sacconi in 1884, and took more than 25 years to complete. Opinions differ as to its architectural and artistic merit but there is no doubting its monumental size and message. At the beginning of the 20th century, the grey structures along the Via Vittorio Veneto were built and set the pattern for many pre-war building projects.

During the Fascist era, a renewed interest in archaeology led to the excavation of many architectural treasures. These in their turn stimulated a new neo-Roman style of which the Foro Italico and the Piazza Augusto Imperiale are typical examples. Under pressure from the growing population, more and more buildings appeared on the right bank of the Tiber in the Prati di Costello and Monteverde quarters and outside the walls in St Giovanni and St Lorenzo. The expansion of the city beyond the walls continued after the Second World War when its population reached two millions.

23

Classical Rome

The Forum Romanum, the centre of Ancient Rome, can be entered through clusters of stallholders and ice cream sellers on the Via dei Fori Imperiali. The Forum was probably first occupied in the sixth century BC after the valley between the Palatine and Capitoline Hills had been drained by the construction of the great sewer called the Cloaca Maxima. Gradually, the shops were removed and the Forum became solely the civic centre of Rome.

Immediately to the right of the entrance are the remains of the Basilica Emilia (179 BC) with its huge central hall. Next door is the Curia where the Roman Senate met from about 650 BC until the fall of the empire. During the Republic, the citizens gathered in the Comitium, the square outside, to make important decisions. At the north-west corner is the Arch of Septimus Severus and in front of what was originally the main square stands the Rostra, a raised dais from which orators like Cicero harangued huge crowds. On the opposite side of the square to the Curia and Basilica Emilia stands the Basilica Julia, which was commissioned by Julius Caesar and served as a court of justice and the Temple of Castor and Pollux (484 BC). The Temple of Julius Caesar forms the fourth side of the square; this was where Caesar's body was burned and Mark Antony gave his famous oration to the people.

From this main square the Via Sacra, the ceremonial thoroughfare, makes its way east, bordered by the Temple of Vesta and the House of the Vestal Virgins on the right and the ruins of the Basilica of Constantine on the left, before passing under the Arch of Titus.

Turning right before the Arch, the visitor can ascend the Clivus Palatinus to the Palatine Hill where, it is said, the first city was laid out by Romulus. Keeping to the left one comes upon the beautifully proportioned Stadium and the ruins of Augustus' and Domitian's great palaces and the House of Livia with its famous murals. From all these sites, there are splendid views out over the Circus Maximus. Immediately to the north lies the Cryptoporticus, a long vaulted passageway which used to connect Nero's Golden House with the Palaces of Augustus, Tiberius and Caligula; the foundations of the last two now lie beneath the Farnese Gardens which can be reached by staircases from the Cryptoporticus.

Outside the Forum Romanum lay five other fora. Nowadays, the Via dei Fori Imperiali on its way to the Colosseum passes the ruins of the Fora of Trajan and Augustus on its left and that of Caesar on its right while crossing over the sites of the Fora of Nerva and Vespasian. At the end of the avenue lies the Colosseum, the greatest testimony to Rome's grandeur and blood lust, with the Arch of Constantine on the right and the remains of Nero's Golden House on the left.

This splendid model by I. Gismondi shows Rome in the days of the Emperor Constantine. On the left, the Circus Maximus stretches alongside the Capitoline, while the Colosseum can be seen on the right.

Left: Originally named the Flavian Amphitheatre, the Colosseum was first referred to by its modern name by the Venerable Bede (673–735) who quoted the prophesy: 'While the Colosseum stands, Rome stands'.

Below: The Palatine seen from the Circus Maximus. Little remains of the giant stadium where crowds numbering 300000 watched chariot races, athletic contests, wild animal shows and sea battles.

Left: These are the remains of the magnificent polychrome marble pavement belonging to the Flavian Palace, part of the Imperial residence on the Palatine.
Right: These three lofty columns are all that remain of the pronaos of the rich and elegant Temple of Vespasian.
Below: Statues of Ancient Rome lining an inner wall just off a busy street.

The Great Basilicas

The basilicas of the Ancient Romans were large buildings used for judicial and other public business. They usually occupied a large site in the Forum. Their design became more or less standardized: a long nave divided by columns into aisles with an apse at the end opposite the entrance. Down to about the end of the tenth century Christians adopted the basilican form for their churches. Among the earliest churches to be erected in Rome were the five great basilicas: St Peter's, St Maria Maggiore, St John Lateran, St Paul's beyond the Walls, and St Lawrence beyond the Walls. These quickly became associated with the Pope and are known as the Five Patriarchical Churches.

St Peter's was built on top of an extensive cemetery on the slopes of the Vatican Hill. Excavations in 1940-1949 uncovered the remains of a pre-Constantinian shrine containing human bones, which appears to have been the object of great veneration. Although this cannot yet be positively identified as St Peter's tomb, it does prove the continuous sanctity of the site from earliest Christian times. The present building is a magnificent concoction produced by Bramante, the first architect, Michelangelo who created the dome and Maderna who designed the nave. Important contributions were also made by many other great artists. The walls and floor of the nave are covered with marble decorations by Giacomo della Porta and Bernini. Among a plethora of splendid works of art, Michelangelo's remarkable Pieta, executed during his early years, is one of the most outstanding.

St Maria Maggiore contains fine fifth-century mosaics above the colonnades of its nave which is decorated with the first gold to have come from America. The baroque facade is by Fuga (1743).

St John Lateran is the metropolitan church of Rome and was rebuilt several times as a result of fires and other disasters until it assumed its present baroque form. The bronze for the great central doors came from the old Roman Senate House in the Forum. Borromini, who refashioned the nave, is responsible for its imposing rather coldly mathematical proportions. The church also contains a statue of Constantine which used to stand in his baths. Adjoining the basilica is the Palazzo del Laterano, the Pope's official residence until the Babylonish Captivity.

According to tradition St Paul is buried beneath St Paul's beyond the Walls. This with the exception of St Peter's, is the largest church in Rome. The original structure was almost completely destroyed by fire in 1823, only the choir and the cloisters escaping the flames. The choir contains 13th-century mosaics and a magnificent altar canopy.

St Lawrence beyond the Walls is the smallest of the Patriarchical churches and is really two churches, one built in the sixth century, the other in the 13th. It contains a fine episcopal throne and excellent pavements in the nave and choir by the famous Cosmati school of Roman artists.

Part of the two semi-circular colonnades which partly enclose the Piazza San Pietro. Each colonnade consists of a quadruple row of Doric columns, forming three parallel covered walks.

Below: The main facade of St Maria Maggiore was designed by Fuga in 1743. It is approached by steps and consists of a portico with a loggia of three arches.
Right: The Basilica of St John Lateran was built in 1574 and is the cathedral of Rome. Until 1870 the Popes were crowned here.

The immensity of the interior of St Peter's is disguised by the symmetry of its proportions. The eye is drawn to Bernini's superb baldacchino which is bathed in light from the great dome.

Left: The facade of St Peter's Basilica. The ballustrade supports statues of Christ, St John the Baptist and eleven of the Apostles – the statue of St Peter is inside.
Below: St Paul's Cloisters were finished in about 1214 and were the work, at least in part, of the Vassalletti. In the centre is a beautiful rose garden.

HIERVSALEM

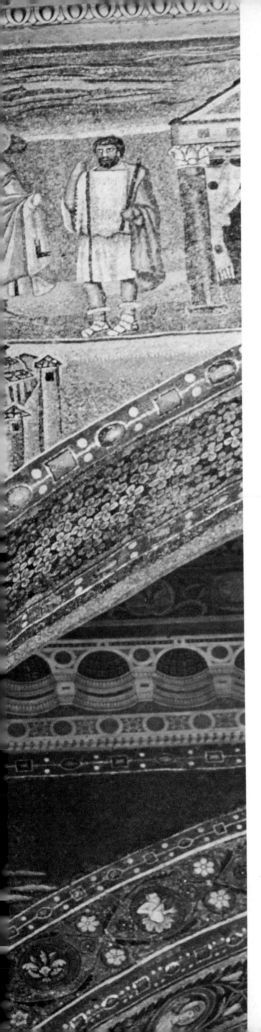

Left: Fine mosaics decorating the sanctuary arch are a striking feature of the interior of St Maria Maggiore. They show lively biblical scenes including the Annunciation, the Visit of the Magi and the Flight into Egypt.

Below: The most famous of Michelangelo's Pietas was completed by the artist in his twenty-fifth year (1499). It is perhaps the most moving of his sculptures and is the only one inscribed with his name.

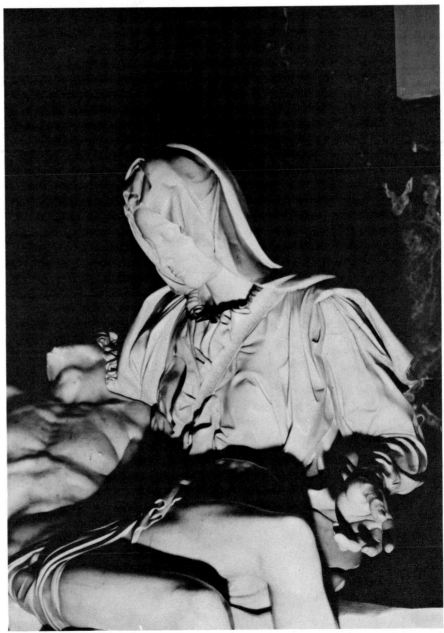

Bridges Over The Tiber

By the end of the Classical Period, five or six bridges had been constructed across the Tiber. Only one now remains more or less intact. The oldest, the Ponte Rotto or the broken bridge, was built in 181 BC but has been extensively restored following serious flood damage in the 16th and 19th centuries. In spite of the constant danger of flooding, it was not until the 19th century that the Lungotevere embankments were built to contain the river and straighten its course.

Further upstream, one comes to the oldest surviving intact bridge, the Ponte Fabricio. It was built in 62 BC and faces the Theatre of Marcellus, one of the finest examples of Roman monumental architecture. The bridge joins the mainland to the almond shaped Isola Tiberina. This island contains the Fatebenefratelli hospital; a tall medieval tower, formerly part of an 11th-century fortress; and the church of St Bartolomeo, which was erected on the site of the temple of Aesculapius. The island is linked to the Trastevere or right bank of the Tiber by the Ponte Cestio which may have been built by the Emperor Gratian. Following the serious 19th-century floods, it had to be entirely rebuilt although the central arch retains its original design and measurements.

The Pons Aelius, now known as the Ponte St Angelo, was built by the Emperor Hadrian in AD 135 as a fitting approach to his great mausoleum. This contained the bodies of many of his successors as well as his own. Only the three central arches of the bridge actually date from this time. Since 1925, the Mausoleum or the Castel St Angelo as it is better known, has been a museum containing a fine collection of weapons dating from the Stone Age to the present day. In addition, the museum boasts some well-known paintings, antique furniture and tapestries.

Some of the finest views in Rome can be seen from the Ponte Umberto, particularly in the early morning light. From the point where the bridge joins the left bank, one can enjoy a magnificent panorama including the Ponte St Angelo, the Castel St Angelo, the Borgo (the walled Leonine city which has been the stronghold of the Papacy since AD 850) and the dome of St Peter's.

The Ponte Cavour joins the main city to the Prati quarter. From it can be seen the Mausoleum of Augustus on the left bank. Augustus, Rome's greatest emperor, and many other members of his family were buried here. Archaeologists unearthed an outer ring of twelve compartments surrounding an inner sepulchral *cella* containing three niches. In the central niche they discovered the cinerary urns of Augustus and his wife Livia with those of his nephews Gaius and Lucius Caesar on one side and that of his sister Octavia on the other. During the Middle Ages, the Colonna made the tomb into a fortress. After various vicissitudes, it became a concert hall and remained as such until 1936.

The last of Rome's great bridges, the Ponte Vittorio Emmanuele, also offers fine views of the city and river, especially at sunset.

The Vatican City lies on the right bank of the Tiber and has the status of an independent state. This is one of the finest views of St Peter's, rising behind the St Angelo Bridge.

Left: Across the bridge lies the Castel St Angelo which was originally the Emperor Hadrian's Mausoleum. Since 1925, it has housed an important collection of military treasures.

Right: The Ponte St Angelo has statues of St Peter and St Paul at the Castel St Angelo end and is lined with ten other statues.

Below: The Ponte Cestio, first built in AD 152, was rebuilt in 1892. It joins the south side of the Isola Tiberina to the Trastevere quarter of Rome.

ASPICIANT·AD·ME
QVEM·C ONFIXERVNT

Left: A single stone arch of the Pons Aemilius, the first stone bridge across the Tiber, remains in the river bed. Since its final collapse in 1598, it has been known as the Ponte Rotto.
Below: The Ponte Umberto I crosses the Tiber between the Castel St Angelo and the Mausoleum of Augustus. It leads to the Palace of Justice on the right bank.

Above left: An elegant new bridge across the Tiber.
Below left: The Ponte Fabrico joins the Isola Tiberina to the left bank of the Tiber.
Above: Another of Rome's many bridges. This one is near St Peter's Square.

Holy Week

The highest point of Rome's year is Holy Week. This is an important family holiday as well as a great religious occasion. For weeks before, the shops are full of gigantic Easter eggs, some fully five feet high and weighing 150 pounds. These spectacular masterpieces of the confectioner's art are usually for decoration rather than for sale – once the festivities are over, they are rendered down into more easily disposable bars.

In the last few days before Easter, pilgrims and tourists pour into the city by car, bus, rail and air. There is usually not a bed to be had in the whole city. On Maundy Thursday, the ceremonies begin with the Mandatum when the Pope washes the feet of twelve old men or twelve young boys, recalling Christ's washing of the disciples' feet. On Good Friday, the service of Tenebrae commemorates the three hours of darkness that fell over the earth following the Crucifixion. One by one the candles in the churches are extinguished until only one bright flame remains alight, representing Christ, the Light of the World. The first Easter Mass is held on Holy Saturday, marking the end of Lent and the churches are full of the pungent smell of incense and crammed with worshippers. On Easter Monday, a quarter of a million people push and shove their way into the Piazza St Pietro, obscuring Bernini's famous fountains to hear the Pope give his traditional blessing, *urbi et orbi,* and to give his Easter message in a variety of languages.

Pilgrims make their way to the five Patriarchical Basilicas and the many other churches, all with their own precious relics. Many visit the Scala Santa, the Sacred Stairs, reputedly those from Pontius Pilate's residence in Jerusalem, down which Christ passed after his condemnation. Thousands ascend these famous 28 steps on their knees, stopping on each to say a prayer. The steps lead to the Chapel of St Lawrence which contains a mosaic of Christ and, protected by a silver tabernacle presented by Innocent III, the relic which gives the chapel its peculiar sanctity.

Meanwhile, many Roman families take the opportunity to set off in cars and buses for their first picnic of the year either at the seaside or in the country. Easter is an exciting time for young children with the giving of presents and sweetmeats. Doting parents take their little ones to see the Punch and Judy shows in the Piazza Navona or the Pincio Gardens.

Pope Paul celebrates Easter and delivers the famous sermon, *urbi et orbi,* from a balcony overlooking St Peter's Square.

Left: Pope Paul being carried through crowds of worshippers to celebrate Mass on Palm Sunday.
Above: A religious co-fraternity leads a procession during Lent.

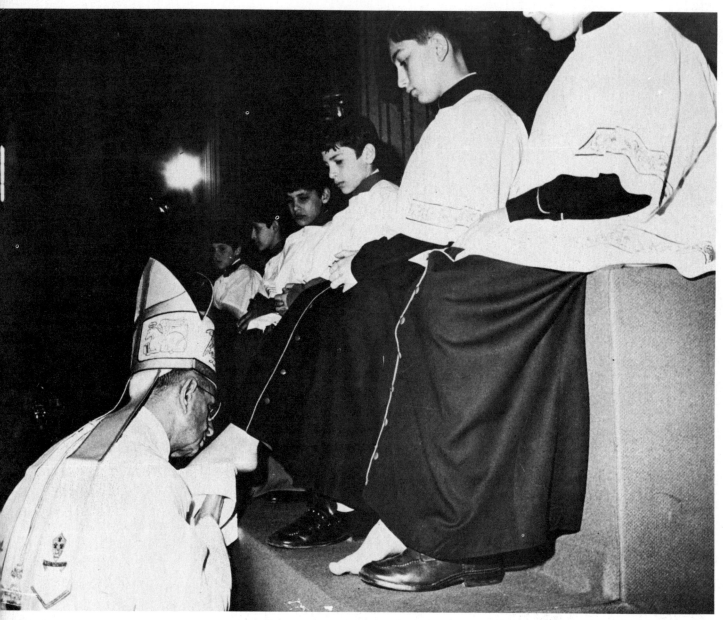

Roman Food and Eating Houses

Food and drink are of absorbing interest to most Romans. Everywhere one goes the streets are full of eating houses: pizzerias, rotisseries, luncheonettes, trattorie and ristoranti offering an amazing variety of meals for every taste and pocket.

Breakfast for visitors usually consists of rolls or crisp bread, butter and conserves although this may be varied at times by the appearance of bomba, excellent jam doughnuts. The Romans usually make do with coffee. The main meals of the day are *pranzo* or dinner, usually eaten between 12.30 pm and 2.30 pm and *cena* or supper, taken at 8.30 pm to 10.30 pm. However, the eating houses and cafes never seem to be empty, just more or less full, as the Romans, like all Italians, are very partial to snacks and glasses of wine, aperitif or liqueur between meals. Certainly, there is nothing more enjoyable after some vigorous sightseeing than sitting in the shade of an awning, sipping a drink and watching the world go by.

Romans' meals are serious, lengthy affairs introduced by antipasti or delicious hors d'oeuvre, soups or pasta. As one would expect every kind of restaurant prides itself on the quality of its spaghetti, cannelloni (rolled pasta pancakes filled with meat, cheese and tomato sauce), lasagne (layers of pasta with a similar filling) and ravioli. Most *trattorie,* the smaller restaurants, offer superb vegetable soups at a very modest price. One of the most popular entrees is paper thin slices of Parma Ham with honey-dew melon or ripe figs.

Probably the best loved of Latin main courses is *Agnello all'aretino,* succulent lamb roasted with rosemary and basted with oil and vinegar, red wine or Marsala. It is cut into thick slices and served in a sauce made from its own juices, with saute potatoes and a green salad. *Porchetta* (roast pork) and *Saltimbocca alla Romana* (slices of veal wrapped around fine strips of prosciutto and sage leaves) are also popular. The main course is usually followed by cheese and fruit although there is normally an extraordinary range of mouthwatering desserts available as well.

Good wines are produced by the neighbouring hill towns. Frascati, Grottaferrata, Albano and Genzano are excellent white wines while Marino and Velletri are the most popular red wines. Most restaurants provide pleasant house wines at reasonable prices. Caffe-espresso, believed to be an aid to digestion, completes a feast fit for a gourmand if not a gourmet.

Although visitors may find the prices charged by the *trattorie* more suited to their pocket, it is well worth paying extra to dine at one of the more expensive restaurants in, say, the Piazza Navona to enjoy the interplay of Italian social life.

Finally, there are a great variety of shops selling sweets, confectionery and ice cream (*gelato*). Without doubt Rome offers a variety and range of food to suit the most discriminating or jaded of palates.

A chef proving, with the help of the maitre d'hotel, that his pasta is good enough to eat.

Below: Music while you eat: small groups of musicians make the rounds of the local restaurants and cafes every lunch and dinner time.
Right: A typical pavement cafe situated in the sidestreets near the Piazza Navona.

Left: Although the way in which meals are presented varies from place to place, the quality remains excellent. The Cafe de Paris in the Via Veneto caters for the smart set.
Below: On a hot summer's night there is nothing quite like a long leisurely dinner in an open-air restaurant.

Right: There are cafes everywhere in Rome. This one is situated in the Piazza del Pantheon.

Above: Eating is a serious business for the Romans. It is a time for conversation and a time for meeting friends.

Right: An empty open-air restaurant is a rare sight in Rome. Only in really cold weather do the regulars take refuge in the interiors of the cafes.

La Dolce Vita

The nature of *La Dolce Vita* in Rome depends very much upon one's financial position. For the rich, the Via Veneto is the centre of Rome's night life, with its nightclubs, bars and restaurants. Otherwise it might be the more intimate parties given in the fashionable residential areas by film stars, politicians and successful businessmen. For them, the winter is a time for visiting fashionable skiing resorts; the summer an opportunity to get away from it all either in their houses up in the hills around Rome, or in their yachts cruising around the Mediterranean. This life is, however, confined to the very few.

For the average Roman, eating-out is an important pastime and there are more than 5000 restaurants to accommodate him. In the suburban quarters, the residents meet at their local cafe to gossip and watch the rest of the world pass by.

For the young Roman the 'passeggio' is the thing. Dressed in their best clothes, they promenade up and down the fashionable piazzas and streets eyeing their contemporaries and criticizing their outfits. The more fortunate young Romans also indulge in the newest version of the passeggio, 'cruising' through the brightly lit streets in their highly polished and decorated cars.

Brought up to believe that the Italian male is probably the world's greatest lover, the young Roman spends a considerable amount of time and money at the barbers – another important Italian meeting place – and the tailors. Dressed to kill, he indulges in the national sport, the pursuit of girls, especially foreigners. Their activities vary from the amusing, for accompanied women, to the frightening for those who are unescorted. Solitary or even group window-shopping and sight-seeing is not to be recommended for female visitors at night.

The Roman spends a good deal of his time either watching or playing sports of one kind or another. Blood sports are still popular. Important boxing matches are held in Rome and the Romans like nothing better than watching two big brave modern-style gladiators thumping each other. Roma, the local football team, inspires fanatical support and the roars of the crowd reach an ear splitting crescendo whenever a match is played.

Betting is a national passion. Billions of lire are spent each week on the football pools, horse and greyhound racing and the national lottery. Betting plays an important part in the life of the poorer Roman: it offers him an opportunity to escape from the mundane day-to-day struggle of work into the elegant and sophisticated world described by gossip columnists and depicted in glossy magazines. As well as all this there are the customary discos and dance halls and more than 200 cinemas, loudly proclaiming their wares from enormous hoardings covered in luridly coloured posters.

The Piazza Barberini is one of the most important squares in Rome. In the centre is Bernini's masterpiece, the Triton Fountain, completed in 1643. The Via Veneto leads from here to the Porta Pinciana.

Left: Two priests on a motor scooter, by no means an unusual sight. The Romans' love affair with all forms of motor transport is as strong as ever.

Above: The open-air Punch and Judy show is a popular attraction during the Easter celebrations with adult and child alike.

Left: Youth waits for age at a street water pump. Signs of poverty can still be seen in what is one of tho world's great cities.
Below: A priest talking to a policeman – the law and the Church are important strands in Roman life.

City of Culture

Rome possesses such a treasury of museums and art galleries that it is difficult to know which to mention and which to leave out. Without doubt the Vatican Palace houses an incomparable series of museums and art galleries. The Museo Paolino contains collections of Roman and neo-Attic sculpture, Christian inscriptions and artefacts from a wide variety of primitive and more recent cultures. The Vatican Picture Gallery covers the whole history of western painting and sculpture from the Byzantine era to the present day. In addition there is the Gallery of Tapestries, the Raphael Rooms and the Sistine Chapel built by Sixtus IV between 1478 and 1481. This, the private chapel of the Popes where the cardinals used to meet to elect the pontiff, is dominated by Michelangelo's masterly ceiling frescoes (1508-1512) telling the Genesis stories from the creation of the world to the adventures of Noah and his vast *Last Judgement* covering the altar wall (1534-1541). The latter became the model for the school of Mannerist painters. Scholars from all over the world visit the Library which contains more than a million printed books and 60000 manuscripts.

The Capitoline Museums contain fine collections of Roman portrait busts, the *Capitoline Venus* and the famous *Dying Goth or Gladiator.* The Picture Gallery of the Palazzo dei Conservatori displays major works by Bellini, Lotto, Veronese, Peruzzi and Titian.

The Galleria Borghese boasts Canova's famous statue of Paolina Borghese, Napoleon's sister, and Bernini's even more renowned *Apollo and Daphne.* The Picture Gallery includes Titian's celebrated *Sacred and Profane Love* among many other masterpieces.

It is not for nothing that St Cecilia, the patron saint of music, was a Roman. Rome has a great reputation for the study and performance of music. Its renowned Academy of St Cecilia was founded by Palestrina and the Rome Opera competes with Milan and Naples for the operatic palm of Italy. During the summer, selections of operas by Verdi, Puccini, Rossini and Donizetti are brilliantly staged at the Baths of Caracalla before huge appreciative crowds. Famous for their stage effects, nothing is more exciting than the chariot charge to the front of the stage in a flash of tossing plumes and shining harness in *Aida.* The ballet and orchestral music are equally popular and open air concerts are often held in the floodlit Basilica of Maxentius in the Roman Forum during the summer.

Rome is also the capital of the Italian film industry – more films are made in Rome than in Hollywood. Forty years ago, the Fascists built a grandiose film city called Cinecittà. In these studios, and the more modern ones on the Via Latina, the likes of Vittorio da Sica, Pier Paolo Pasolini, Dino de Laurentiis, Ponti and Zeffirelli have produced some of Italy's finest films.

Rome possesses Italy's largest university and attracts students and scholars from all over the world because of its excellent facilities and high academic standards.

Michelangelo's statue of Moses in St Peter's in Chains. This powerful figure was one of several planned by Michelangelo for Julius II's tomb, but the rest were never finished.

70

Left: Trajan's column is 97 feet high and made of 18 drums of marble. A spiral frieze winds around the column covered with 2500 figures illustrating the Emperor's Dacian campaign.

Above: Hundreds of ancient statues have been unearthed during excavations. In spite of many years' work, there is still a wealth of artefacts to be discovered.

The *School of Athens* by Raphael in
the Vatican Palace represents the
triumph of philosophy. Plato and
Aristotle dominate the scene and
are surrounded by groups of the
world's greatest scholars.
Overleaf: The Creation of Adam,
perhaps the most famous scene
from Michelangelo's frescoes on
the ceiling of the Sistine Chapel.
They were painted between 1508
and 1512.

Squares and Fountains

Rome is a city of squares which resound to the lapping and bubbling of water and whose walls reflect its myriad lights. The building and adorning of fountains is an old Roman tradition. It is claimed that Imperial Rome contained no less that 1352 fountains. Their greatest post-classical creator was Lorenzo Bernini. It is believed that he was responsible for the original plans of the Trevi Fountains which form one whole facade of the Palazzo Poli and represent the royal residence of Neptune, god of the sea.

The River Fountain in the Piazza Navona is one of Bernini's finest works, and was executed by the master and his students between 1647 and 1650. The four magnificent statues represent the rivers Danube, Ganges, Nile and Rio de la Plata. The Piazza has retained the shape of the Emperor Domitian's stadium and racecourse upon which it is built. Throughout Rome's history, festivals, jousts and open air sports have been held here. From the 17th to the 19th century, the Romans crowded to the square on every Saturday in August to see it turned into a shallow lake of sparkling, prismatic coloured waters. It is still the most animated piazza in Rome and contains some of its finest and best loved ristoranti.

The Piazza Barberini is one of the most important squares in Rome. In its centre stands Bernini's masterpiece, the Fontana del Tritone (1642-1643). Four dolphins support a shell upon which a triton is seated blowing water out through a conch shell held between his hands.

The Piazza del Popolo, designed by Valadier in 1814, forms the most noble and impressive entrance to Rome. At its centre stands an ancient Egyptian obelisk which is guarded by four lion fountains, created by Valadier. The hieroglyphics on the obelisk tell of the bloody victories of the Pharaohs, Ramses II and Merenptah in the second millenium BC. Augustus brought the monument back to Rome and set it up in the Circus Maximus, the great racetrack lying in the shadow of the Palatine Hill. It was removed to its present site in the 16th century as part of the ambitious urban plans of Sixtus V.

Another renowned centre is the Piazza di Spagna containing the Spanish Steps where, in the old days, artist's models used to ply for hire. This was the heart of romantic Rome when it was frequented by people like Gogol, Stendhal, Liszt and D'Annunzio, the poet-soldier Mussolini modelled himself upon. In 1821, John Keats died in the red house at the bottom of the steps; this is now a museum in his honour. Every day, the foot of the steps is covered by a gorgeous selection of flowers for sale. But they are seen at their finest at the beginning of May when they are decorated with tubs of magnificent azaleas.

Every visitor to Rome will carry away his own kaleidoscope of memories of the many squares and fountains he has encountered in the course of his travels through the city. He will probably agree with the Ancient Romans who said that *Murmure suo fons canit vitae laudem* – by its murmuring the fountain sings the praise of life.

The Spanish Steps. This famous flight of 137 steps was built in 1721–1725. On top of the steps, the Piazza della Trinita dei Monte is dominated by an ancient obelisk and the church of the same name.

Below: The Fountain of Rivers by Bernini has a colossal statue at each corner representing the rivers Danube, Ganges, Nile and Plate. Here, the Nile covers its face.

Right: A view of the Piazza Navona. In the foreground, Neptune struggles with a sea monster, surrounded by nereids and sea horses, in a fountain designed by Leone della Bitta and Zappola in 1878.

From the roof of St Peter's one can see the full glory of Bernini's colonnades which open so that the eye looks down the Via della Conciliazone to the Tiber and the Castel St Angelo.

Above: The splendid fountains at the centre of the Piazza della Rotonda emerge from this elaborate base. Above it rises the obelisk of Rameses the Great which used to grace the Temple of Isis.

Below: Steps leading to the Capitoline Hill or the Campidoglio, the smallest but most famous of the Seven Hills of Rome. The Palazzo Senatorio, behind, was the official seat of the Governor of Rome.

Left: The Fountains of Trevi were completed in 1762. Two giant Tritons lead Neptune's winged chariot while the figures of Abundance and Health stand in niches on either side.

Below: The Piazza della Bocca della Verita occupies part of the ancient cattle market of Rome. In the background stands the Temple of Vesta.

Stores and Markets

Rome's most famous shopping areas are not as dominated by great department stores as those of Paris or London. The Romans prefer smaller, more personal, specialist shops. Where department stores exist in the centre of Rome they still exude a faint aura of better days with their rather opulent, faded style of exterior decoration. The memory of these rather Edwardian structures vividly contrasts with the bright and sometimes rather tawdry department stores and supermarkets of the new residential quarters.

Although the Via del Corso stretching from the Vittoriano to the Piazza del Popolo and the Via Veneto are reputedly the best shopping areas, the finest and indeed the most expensive shops are to be found in the little streets off the Corso especially the Via Condotti which leads to the Piazza di Spagna and the Spanish Steps. Here window shoppers can see the finest and most expensive goods produced in Italy and the rest of the world. Particularly attractive are the jewellers with their collections of rings, bracelets and necklaces set with crystals, corals, ivories and jades as well as the more conventional precious stones. Every shop has in addition a wide selection of cameos. For the visitor, the best buys are leather goods – the shoes, sandals and gloves are particularly good – and the splendid silk shirts, ties and scarves which are available in every shade of colour and style.

Excellent small shops can also be found in the Piazza del Parlamento and the Via della Scrofa near the Piazza Navona. Fine clothes for children and adults are readily available at a price. It should not be forgotten that Rome is one of the great fashion capitals of the world and is well known for its well cut and often daring creations. Genuine and astronomically expensive antiques are for sale in the Via del Babuino and the Via del Coronari.

Rome is not short of markets. Every day, in one quarter at least, there is a full scale market as well as the permanent ones at the Piazza Vittorio Emmanuele II, the Campo dei Fiori and the Porta Portese. The latter is the site of Rome's Flea Market where almost anything can be bought from junk, genuine antiques, cheap clothes, flowers from the Alban Hills and fish from Ostia. These open air markets are dominated by the bawling of the street vendors and the hubbub of the traffic.

Every square has its own food and vegetable stalls and flower sellers who sprinkle the dusty pavements in summer with cooling water; the scent of whose produce sweetens the otherwise rather rank smell. The best place to buy flowers is still the Spanish Steps in the Piazza di Spagna. Everywhere one goes there are ever-ready ice cream and mineral water sellers.

A sausage stall. Everywhere one goes in Rome, there are food stalls, festooned with mouth-watering delicacies.

Left: A shoe shop in the Via Veneto. Even Rome's smartest streets cater for all pockets.
Above: A clothes stall in an open-air market. Like every great European capital, Rome has its flea market.

Left: During the summer, flower stalls provide a welcome patch of colour and a source of sweet scents in many a dusty Roman Street.

Below left: Some Romans insist on doing all their shopping in the open markets where they can enjoy the delights of haggling over every price.

Below: A vegetable stall offering a comprehensive selection of Mediterranean produce.

Above: The Campo dei Fiori is an attractive market with old stalls and canvas shades. At one time, this was where public executions were held.
Right: Ready for the pot. Live chickens in an open-air market.

Roman Excursions

Many places of interest lie within easy reach of Rome. One of the most beautiful is Hadrian's Villa, situated on hill slopes planted with olives, stone pines and cypresses some three miles from Tivoli. Little is now left of the vast palace the emperor built as a refuge from the cares of office. Originally it contained copies of many of the buildings he had seen and admired on his journeys around the empire. Of these all that remains are fine examples of the Roman theatre and baths, giving the visitor some idea of the luxury and grandeur that Hadrian enjoyed.

Tivoli itself is a pleasant summer resort, chiefly famous for the Villa d'Este which dates from the 1550s and is situated in a magnificent terraced garden containing 500 fountains. At the lower end of the town on the banks of the River Anio, one of the chief tributaries of the Tiber, stands the Temple of Vesta, which was admired by the Renaissance masters including Bramante whose Tempietto was, it is argued, inspired by its study.

Frascati, on the vine clad slopes of the Alban Hills, was once the home of Henry, Cardinal of York, the younger brother of Charles Edward Stuart, Bonnie Prince Charlie. The town's main attractions are its baroque cathedral and its famous white wines. The next villages along the road, Montepozio and Montecompatri, command fine views over Tivoli to the Sabine Hills. From the motorway and from the old Roman track beneath it, visitors can enjoy magnificent panoramas of the Monti Prenestini to the east.

Tusculum, another fine hill town, older than Rome itself, offers fine prospects of the whole of the Campagna to the capital and the sea beyond, the Sabine Hills and Monte Cavo, the highest of the Alban Hills. During the Middle Ages, the town served as a fortress for the local counts who made the mistake of espousing the cause of the Hohenstauffen Holy Roman Emperors from Germany. This led in 1191 to the whole town being systematically destroyed by order of the vengeful Roman senate. Hardly anything remains of the medieval and classical buildings that once lined its streets.

A short bus ride away from the capital lies Ariccia and Bernini's church, St Maria Assunta. Further along the road, the traveller comes upon Lake Albano at whose southwestern corner, high on the slopes of the hills and approached by a great avenue of ilex trees, stands a Capuchin monastery. From this vantage point, one can look across the lake to the site of prehistoric Alba Longa. It is only a short journey from here to Castel Gandolfo which contains the Pope's summer residence and St Tommaso, another beautiful domed church by Bernini.

Within easy reach of Rome by the Metropolitana (the local electric railway) or by bus are the ruins of Ostia, the ancient port of Rome. Here one can see one of the most complete ground plans of a Roman town ever excavated.

Ostia Antica is the ancient port of Rome. It is named after the ostium or mouth of the river Tiber.

Above: The villa d'Este has incomparable gardens and 500 fountains. They contrast vividly with their parched surroundings.

Below: The Pope's summer
residence at Castel Gandolfo
overlooks Lake Albano. The palace,
its gardens and the former Villa
Barberini enjoy the privilege of
extra-territoriality.

Left and right: Ostia once supported a population of 100000 devoted to satisfying the needs of the capital. Excavations have revealed its complete ground plan. It was divided into housing blocks by straight streets which intersected at right angles. There are good examples of fora, temples, theatres and even a fire station.

Below: Many fine mosaics in black and white stone have also been discovered at Ostia.